1000 Fences and Gates

BEWARE OF DOG

Jo Cryder

Schiffer Publishing Ltd

4880 Lower Valley Road, Atglen, PA 19310 USA

Designed by Mark David Bowyer
Type set in Zapf Humanist BT / Aldine 721 BT

ISBN: 0-7643-2409-8
Printed in China

Published by Schiffer Publishing Ltd.
4880 Lower Valley Road
Atglen, PA 19310
Phone: (610) 593-1777; Fax: (610) 593-2002
E-mail: Info@schifferbooks.com

For the largest selection of fine reference books on this and related subjects, please visit our web site at **www.schifferbooks.com**
We are always looking for people to write books on new and related subjects. If you have an idea for a book please contact us at the above address.

This book may be purchased from the publisher.
Include $3.95 for shipping.
Please try your bookstore first.
You may write for a free catalog.

In Europe, Schiffer books are distributed by
Bushwood Books
6 Marksbury Ave.
Kew Gardens
Surrey TW9 4JF England
Phone: 44 (0) 20 8392-8585; Fax: 44 (0) 20 8392-9876
E-mail: info@bushwoodbooks.co.uk
Free postage in the U.K., Europe; air mail at cost.

Contents

Author's Note: Shortly after this book was submitted to the publisher, Hurricanes Katrina and Rita devastated New Orleans, Biloxi, Mobile, and other areas along the Gulf Coast where many of the fences and gates for this book were photographed. While the fate of each location shown is unknown, their depiction here is a bittersweet reminder of the many beautiful properties that once graced these areas…and hopefully will again.

Preface

San Diego, California has been my home for more than thirty years. It's a wonderful place to live, but during the summer of 2004 I decided I wanted to travel throughout the United States and experience living in other places. I work as a stock photographer when I'm in San Diego and also do custom picture framing. This trip would give me the opportunity to add more photos to my stock of pictures.

I rented out my home and left San Diego September 9, 2004. I traveled north to Washington State, then east to Wisconsin where I turned south with the idea of settling in the Florida Keys for the winter months. This is where I was located when I started collecting pictures of fences and gates. As it turned out, all of the pictures in this book were taken between April and July of 2005.

Come with me as I travel from the Florida Keys to the following areas, photographing the fences and gates along the way: Jacksonville, Florida; Atlanta, Georgia; Chattanooga, Tennessee; Asheville, North Carolina; Sumter, Myrtle Beach, and Charleston, South Carolina. We then head west along Florida's panhandle coast into Mobile, Alabama, and Mississippi, ending my westward journey in New Orleans. Then north in Mississippi to include cities like Natchez, Vicksburg, Jackson, Canton, Kosciuski, Tupelo, and Nesbit. From Memphis I turned east to Nashville, Tennessee. I finished the trip going from Tennessee into Virginia, Washington, D.C., and ending in Pennsylvania.

Interesting fences and gates were targeted for picture taking, including those at famous places I visited along the way. If available, I have included information about these places as well as websites where additional information about them can be found. Other fences and gates are located at the homes of well-known people, and if I know who they are I identify them. Most of the time, however, the residents of the homes where I took pictures were unknown to me.

The fences and gates have been sorted by type of material, including metal, stone, masonry, concrete, wood, and combinations thereof. Just looking at the pictures, it isn't always obvious what materials were used. Chapter 6 features a variety of fences and gates photographed at places of special interest.

At times, it may look like the pictures were taken at odd angles. This is because every effort was made to avoid vehicles, garbage cans, telephone poles, wiring, and people. Sometimes the home, building, garden, or other element of the property was intentionally included in order to show the overall effect of adding fences and gates.

All of the pictures are meant to show style, beauty, function, and—most of all—possibilities. You will find this wonderful assortment of fences and gates valuable in many ways:

- As a homeowner, you are considering adding a fence and/or gate to your property.
- Security is a concern and you want to see how others have dealt with enclosing their property.
- You have or want to build a garden and need something to pull it all together.
- You have just built or remodeled your home and want to set it apart from other homes in the area.
- A fence and gate are required around a swimming pool and/or hot tub.
- You have children or pets that need to be confined.
- You are a contractor or landscaper who designs, builds, and/or remodels fences and gates.

Some fences and gates seem to say "we, the owners, are proud of our property"… they've been used to decorate and to make visitors feel welcome while still providing security. Others surround the property completely and seem to convey, "All this is my property," or "Respect our privacy and stay out unless invited." Some are expressions of artistic décor, the finishing touches to a blissful sanctuary. As you turn these pages, you'll see gates without fences, fences without gates, and, in some cases, just a decoration that shows a desire to make the area special and provide a welcoming approach to the property.

I hope you enjoy viewing these photographs as much as I enjoyed taking them!

Acknowledgments

In spite of the fact that I traveled alone, I was not always alone. There were many people along the way that assisted in finding exceptional opportunities for photography. Their efforts in guiding me—often physically driving me in their vehicles—to the locations of fences and gates made it possible to include subjects I would not have otherwise known about or known how to locate. My gratitude and thanks to all of the following: Dick Alexander in the Florida Keys and Myrtle Beach, South Carolina, helped me kick off the project by locating the first fences and gates to be photographed. Bill and Sally Ryan chauffeured me around Jacksonville to the many special locations in that city. Their son, Bill, and wife Allison Ryan put their Humvee and knowledge of the area to use as we sought out beauties in Atlanta, Georgia. Gloria Nixon and I explored the streets, roads, summits, and parks of Chattanooga and Nashville, Tennessee, in her SUV and found many of the fences and gates there, including those of country music fame. Sandra Tegland maneuvered around Washington, D.C., making it possible for me to photograph fences and gates in high traffic areas. All of you are still contributing moral support and well wishes for the success of this book. I want you to know how much I appreciate and thank each of you. I also want to thank all of the other people, too numerous to mention, who assisted me as I visited their areas of the country. These are the people who went out of their way to give me directions, ideas, and reference materials that assisted me in my search. Most of all, gracious thanks to Nancy Schiffer and Schiffer Publishing Ltd. for this tremendous opportunity to produce my first published, exclusive collection of photographs. May this be the first of many more.

Chapter 1
Metal Fences and Gates
Combined with Stone, Masonry, or Concrete

Florida Keys

Florida Keys

Florida Keys

Florida Keys

Florida Keys

Florida Keys

Florida Keys

Florida Keys

Florida Keys

Florida Keys

Florida Keys

Florida Keys

Florida Keys

Florida Keys

Florida Keys

Florida Keys

Florida Keys

Florida Keys

Florida Keys

Florida Keys

Jacksonville, Florida

Florida Keys

Jacksonville, Florida

Jacksonville, Florida

Jacksonville, Florida

Jacksonville, Florida

Jacksonville, Florida

Jacksonville, Florida

Jacksonville, Florida

Jacksonville, Florida

South Carolina

Swan Lake Iris Gardens

Swan Lake and the surrounding Iris Gardens are scenic places to visit and to see the hundred-foot-high leaf pine, the cypress trees in the lake and swamp areas, and the different kinds of swans, ducks, geese, and herons that live on the lake. In May, 6,000,000 Japanese iris bloom along with other varieties of flowers.

Website: http://167.7.8.69/iris.html

Sumter, South Carolina – Swan Lake Iris Gardens

Sumter, South Carolina –
Swan Lake Iris Gardens

Sumter, South Carolina – Swan Lake Iris Gardens

Sumter, South Carolina – Swan Lake Iris Gardens

Sumter, South Carolina – Swan Lake Iris Gardens

Sumter, South Carolina –
Swan Lake Iris Gardens

Sumter, South Carolina

Sumter, South Carolina

Sumter, South Carolina – YMCA

Sumter, South Carolina – YMCA, childcare enclosure

Atlanta, Georgia – Georgia Governor's
Executive Mansion

Atlanta, Georgia

Atlanta, Georgia

Atlanta, Georgia

Atlanta, Georgia

Atlanta, Georgia

The Biltmore

In 2005, the Biltmore Estate announced its celebration of the 75th anniversary of Biltmore House opening to the public. America's largest home was completed in 1895, and today it offers a glimpse back to a world of elegance, beauty, and grandeur. The 250-room chateau is filled with treasures collected during George Vanderbilt's world travels.

Website: www.biltmore.com

Asheville, North Carolina – The Biltmore Estate

Asheville, North Carolina – The Biltmore Estate

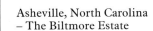

Asheville, North Carolina – The Biltmore Estate

South Carolina

Myrtle Beach, South Carolina

South Carolina

Myrtle Beach, South Carolina

South Carolina

Myrtle Beach, South Carolina

Myrtle Beach, South Carolina

Myrtle Beach, South Carolina

Myrtle Beach, South Carolina

Myrtle Beach, South Carolina

Myrtle Beach, South Carolina

Myrtle Beach, South Carolina

Myrtle Beach,
South Carolina

Myrtle Beach, South Carolina

Myrtle Beach, South Carolina

Myrtle Beach, South Carolina

Myrtle Beach, South Carolina

Myrtle Beach, South Carolina

Myrtle Beach, South Carolina

Georgetown, South Carolina

Georgetown, South Carolina

Georgetown, South Carolina

Georgetown, South Carolina

Georgetown, South Carolina

Georgetown, South Carolina

Charleston, South Carolina

Charleston, South Carolina

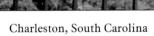

Charleston, South Carolina

Charleston, South Carolina

Charleston, South Carolina

Charleston, South Carolina

Charleston, South Carolina

Charleston, South Carolina

Charleston, South Carolina

Charleston,
South Carolina

Charleston, South Carolina

Charleston, South Carolina

Charleston, South Carolina

Charleston, South Carolina

Charleston, South Carolina

Charleston,
South
Carolina

Charleston,
South Carolina

Charleston, South Carolina

Charleston, South Carolina

Charleston, South Carolina

Charleston, South Carolina

Charleston, South Carolina

Charleston, South Carolina

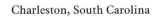

Charleston, South Carolina

Charleston, South Carolina

Charleston,
South Carolina

26

Charleston, South Carolina

Charleston,
South Carolina

Charleston, South Carolina

Charleston, South Carolina

Charleston, South Carolina

Charleston, South Carolina

Charleston, South
Carolina

Charleston, South Carolina

Charleston, South Carolina

Charleston, South Carolina

Charleston, South Carolina

Charleston,
South
Carolina

Charleston, South Carolina

Charleston, South Carolina

Charleston, South Carolina

Charleston,
South Carolina

Charleston,
South Carolina

Charleston,
South Carolina

Charleston, South Carolina

Charleston, South Carolina

Charleston, South Carolina

Charleston, South Carolina

Charleston, South Carolina

Charleston,
South Carolina

Charleston, South Carolina

DOG
Please
Close Gate!

Charleston, South Carolina

Charleston, South Carolina

Charleston, South Carolina

Charleston, South Carolina

Charleston, South Carolina

Charleston, South Carolina

Charleston, South Carolina

Charleston, South Carolina

Charleston, South Carolina

Charleston, South Carolina

Charleston,
South
Carolina

Charleston,
South Carolina

34

Charleston, South Carolina

Charleston, South Carolina

Charleston, South Carolina

Charleston,
South Carolina

Charleston,
South Carolina

Charleston, South Carolina

Charleston, South Carolina

Charleston, South Carolina

Charleston, South Carolina

Charleston, South
Carolina

Charleston, South Carolina

Charleston, South Carolina

Charleston, South Carolina

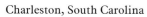

Charleston,
South Carolina

Charleston, South Carolina

Charleston, South Carolina

Charleston, South Carolina

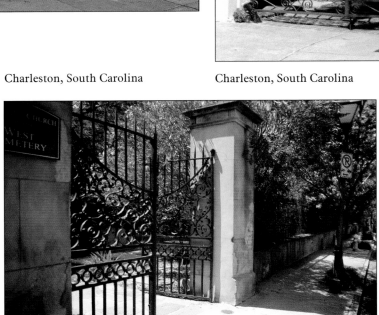

Charleston, South Carolina

Charleston, South Carolina

Charleston,
South Carolina

Charleston, South Carolina

Charleston, South Carolina

Charleston, South Carolina

Charleston, South Carolina

Charleston, South Carolina

Charleston,
South Carolina

Charleston, South Carolina

40

Charleston, South Carolina

Charleston,
South
Carolina

Charleston, South Carolina

Charleston, South Carolina

Charleston,
South Carolina

Charleston, South Carolina

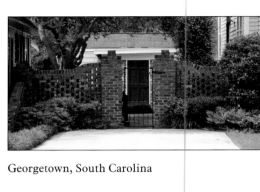

Georgetown, South Carolina

Charleston, South Carolina

Charleston, South
Carolina

South Carolina

Georgetown, South Carolina

Georgetown, South Carolina

Georgetown, South Carolina

Georgetown,
South Carolina

Georgetown, South Carolina

Georgetown, South Carolina

Georgetown, South Carolina

Georgetown, South Carolina

Georgetown, South Carolina

St. George Island, Florida

St. George Island, Florida

Georgetown, South Carolina

St. George Island, Florida

St. George Island, Florida

Mobile, Alabama

Mobile, Alabama

St. George Island, Florida

Mobile, Alabama

Panama City Beach, Florida

Panama City Beach, Florida

Mobile, Alabama – Fort Conde Welcome
Center and Historic Museum

Fort Conde Welcome Center and Historic Museum

Fort Conde Welcome Center and Historic Museum in Mobile offers information and sightseeing possibilities in this historic city. There is also the opportunity of a free tour of Fort Conde, a replica of the original eighteenth century French fort.

Mobile, Alabama – Fort Conde Welcome Center and Historic Museum

Mobile, Alabama – Fort Conde Welcome Center and Historic Museum

Mobile, Alabama – Fort Conde Welcome Center and Historic Museum

47

Mobile, Alabama

Mobile, Alabama

Mobile, Alabama

Dauphin Island, Alabama

New Orleans, Louisiana – Lafayette Cemetery No. 1 located within the Garden District

New Orleans, Louisiana – Lafayette Cemetery No. 1 located within the Garden District

New Orleans, Louisiana – Lafayette Cemetery No. 1 located within the Garden District

New Orleans, Louisiana – Garden District

New Orleans, Louisiana – Garden District

New Orleans, Louisiana – Garden District

New Orleans, Louisiana – Garden District

New Orleans,
Louisiana –
Garden District

New Orleans, Louisiana
– Garden District

New Orleans, Louisiana – Garden District

New Orleans, Louisiana
– Garden District

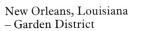

New Orleans, Louisiana – Garden District

New Orleans, Louisiana – Garden District

New Orleans, Louisiana
– Garden District

New Orleans, Louisiana – Garden District

New Orleans,
Louisiana – Garden
District

New Orleans, Louisiana – Garden District

New Orleans, Louisiana – Garden District

New Orleans, Louisiana – Garden District

New Orleans, Louisiana – Garden District

New Orleans, Louisiana
– Garden District

New Orleans, Louisiana – Garden District

New Orleans, Louisiana – Garden District

New Orleans, Louisiana – Garden District

New Orleans, Louisiana – Garden District

New Orleans, Louisiana – Garden District

Louisiana

New Orleans, Louisiana – Garden District

Louisiana

Louisiana

Louisiana, near New Orleans

Louisiana

Natchez, Mississippi

Natchez, Mississippi

Natchez,
Mississippi

Natchez, Mississippi

Natchez, Mississippi

Natchez, Mississippi

Natchez, Mississippi

Natchez, Mississippi

56

Natchez, Mississippi

Natchez, Mississippi

Natchez, Mississippi

Natchez, Mississippi

Natchez, Mississippi

Natchez, Mississippi

Natchez, Mississippi

Natchez, Mississippi

Natchez, Mississippi

Natchez, Mississippi

Natchez, Mississippi

Jackson, Mississippi

Vicksburg, Mississippi

Natchez, Mississippi

Vicksburg, Mississippi

Vicksburg, Mississippi

Vicksburg, Mississippi

Canton, Mississippi

Canton, Mississippi

Canton, Mississippi

Canton, Mississippi

Canton, Mississippi

Canton, Mississippi

Kosciuski, Mississippi

Kosciuski, Mississippi

Memphis, Tennessee

Memphis, Tennessee

Tupelo, Mississippi

Tupelo, Mississippi

Memphis, Tennessee

Chattanooga, Tennessee

Nashville, Tennessee – entrance to the home of singer Jimmy Reeves

Nashville, Tennessee – entrance to the home of singer Jimmy Reeves

Chattanooga, Tennessee

Nashville, Tennessee – entrance to the home of singer Jimmy Reeves

Nashville, Tennessee – State Capitol Building

Nashville, Tennessee – Governor's Executive Mansion

Nashville, Tennessee
– Governor's
Executive Mansion

Nashville, Tennessee – State Capitol Building

The Governor's executive residence is a private residence purchased by the State of Tennessee in 1948 to serve as the official residence of the Governor of Tennessee.

Nashville,
Tennessee –
Governor's
Executive
Mansion

Nashville, Tennessee –
Governor's Executive Mansion

Nashville, Tennessee

Nashville, Tennessee – Vanderbilt University

Nashville, Tennessee

Nashville, Tennessee – Vanderbilt University

Nashville, Tennessee

Nashville, Tennessee – "Starstruck" ranch

Nashville, Tennessee – entrance to the home of Reba McEntire (www.reba.com)

Nashville, Tennessee – "Starstruck" ranch

Nashville, Tennessee – entrance to the home of Marty Stuart (www.martystuart.net)

Nashville, Tennessee – "Starstruck" ranch

Nashville, Tennessee – entrance to the home of Marty Stuart

Nashville, Tennessee – entrance to the home of Roy Orbison (www.orbison.com)

Nashville, Tennessee – entrance to the home of Roy Orbison

Nashville, Tennessee –
entrance to the home
of Roy Orbison

Nashville, Tennessee – entrance to the home of Johnny Cash

Nashville, Tennessee – entrance to
the home of Johnny Cash
(www.johnnycash.com)

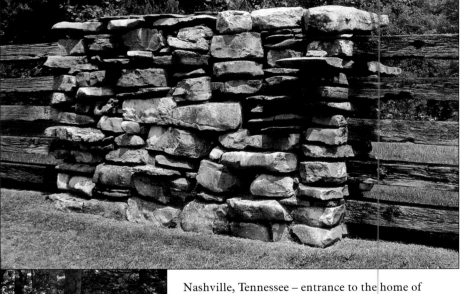

Nashville, Tennessee –
entrance to the home of
Johnny Cash

Nashville, Tennessee –
entrance to the home of
Johnny Cash

Nashville, Tennessee – entrance to the home of
Johnny Cash

Nashville, Tennessee

Nashville, Tennessee

Nashville, Tennessee

Nashville, Tennessee – entrance to the
home of Little Jimmy Dickens
(www.littlejimmydickens.com)

Nashville, Tennessee –Tom T. Hall's home

Nashville, Tennessee

Nashville, Tennessee – George Jones' home

Nashville, Tennessee – George Jones' home

Nashville, Tennessee

Nashville, Tennessee

Nashville, Tennessee – entrance to Tanya Tucker's ranch (www.tanyatucker.com)

Nashville, Tennessee

Nashville, Tennessee

Nashville, Tennessee

Nashville, Tennessee

Nashville, Tennessee

Washington, D.C.

Washington, D.C.

Washington, D.C.

Washington, D.C.

Washington, D.C.

Chapter 2

Metal Fences and Gates

The Museum of Mobile

The Museum of Mobile is housed in a building constructed in 1857 and presents exhibits of Native American, Colonial, African-American, and antebellum influences. It is conveniently located across from the Fort Conde Welcome Center and Historic Museum.

Website: www.museumofmobile.com

Orlando, Florida

Orlando, Florida

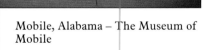

Mobile, Alabama – The Museum of Mobile

Mobile, Alabama – The Museum of Mobile

Mobile, Alabama – The Museum of Mobile

Mobile, Alabama – The Museum of Mobile

Mobile, Alabama – The Museum of Mobile

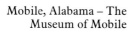

Mobile, Alabama – The Museum of Mobile

Mobile, Alabama – The Museum of Mobile

Mobile, Alabama

Mobile, Alabama

Mobile, Alabama

Mobile, Alabama

New Orleans, Louisiana – Garden District

Mobile, Alabama – USS Alabama Battleship Memorial Park (www.ussalabama.com)

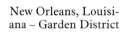

New Orleans, Louisiana – Garden District

Biloxi, Mississippi

New Orleans, Louisiana – Garden District

New Orleans, Louisiana – Garden District

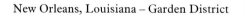

Ormond Plantation

Constructed circa 1787, Ormond Plantation is listed in the National Register of Historic Places. It offers daily tours and overnight accommodations, complete with plantation-style breakfast.

Website: www.plantation.com

Canton, Mississippi

The City of Canton, Mississippi is the site of the Jake Brigance Law Office in the movie *A Time to Kill*, based on the novel by Mississippi author John Grisham.

Canton, Mississippi

Destrehan, Louisiana – Ormond Plantation

Destrehan, Louisiana – Ormond Plantation

Canton, Mississippi

Oak Alley Plantation

This working sugar plantation, circa 1839, is famous for its quarter-mile long alley of evenly spaced, three hundred year old oak trees. It is open daily.

Website: www.oakalleyplantation.com

Canton, Mississippi

Vacherie, Louisiana –
Oak Alley Plantation

Canton, Mississippi

Mississippi

Brentwood, Tennessee – entrance to home of Dolly Parton

Charlottesville, Virginia – Michie Tavern, c. 1784. Michie Tavern is located near Monticello.

Charlottesville, Virginia – Michie Tavern

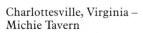

Washington, D.C. – this and the following four photos were taken along what is locally known as "Embassy Row."

Washington, D.C.

Washington, D.C.

Washington, D.C.

Washington, D.C.

Washington, D.C.

Orlando, Florida

Florida Keys

Charleston, South Carolina

Mobile, Alabama

Florida Keys

St. George Island, Florida

Mobile, Alabama

Mobile, Alabama

Bellingrath Gardens

Bellingrath Gardens has a heart-warming history that can be found on the website below. Located more than twenty-four miles from downtown Mobile, it is a favorite destination of visitors to southern Alabama.

Website: www.bellingrath.org

Theodore, Alabama – Bellingrath Gardens

Theodore, Alabama – Bellingrath Gardens

New Orleans, Louisiana

New Orleans, Louisiana

New Orleans, Louisiana

New Orleans, Louisiana

New Orleans, Louisiana

New Orleans, Louisiana

New Orleans, Louisiana

New Orleans, Louisiana

New Orleans, Louisiana

New Orleans, Louisiana

Natchez, Mississippi

New Orleans, Louisiana

Natchez, Mississippi

New Orleans, Louisiana

Tennessee

Nashville, Tennessee

Chapter 3
Stone, Masonry, or Concrete Fences

Florida Keys

Georgetown, South
Carolina

Charleston, South Carolina

Georgetown, South Carolina

Mobile, Alabama

Mobile, Alabama

Charleston, South Carolina

South Carolina

South Carolina

New Orleans, Louisiana

New Orleans, Louisiana

Natchez, Mississippi – Plantation Campground

Florida Keys

Florida Keys

Florida Keys

Jacksonville, Florida

Jacksonville, Florida

Lookout
Mountain,
Tennessee

Jacksonville, Florida

Lookout Mountain, Tennessee

Myrtle Beach, South Carolina

Myrtle Beach, South Carolina

South Carolina

Myrtle Beach, South Carolina

Myrtle Beach,
South Carolina

90

Myrtle Beach, South Carolina

Myrtle Beach, South Carolina

Myrtle Beach, South Carolina

Charleston, South Carolina

Charleston, South Carolina

Charleston, South
Carolina

Charleston, South
Carolina

Charleston, South Carolina

Charleston, South Carolina

Charleston, South Carolina

Georgetown,
South Carolina

Georgetown,
South Carolina

Georgetown, South Carolina

Georgetown,
South Carolina

St. George Island, Florida

Dauphin Island, Alabama

New Orleans,
Louisiana

Canton, Mississippi

94

Canton, Mississippi

Nashville, Tennessee

Memphis, Tennessee

95

Chapter 4

Wood or Wood Appearing Fences and Gates

Florida

Florida

Orlando, Florida

Florida

Orlando, Florida

Orlando, Florida

Sunset Key,
Florida

Orlando, Florida

Sunset Key, Florida

Orlando, Florida

Orlando, Florida

97

Carrabelle Beach, Florida

Charleston,
South Carolina

Georgetown, South Carolina

Charleston, South Carolina

98

Charleston, South Carolina

Charleston, South Carolina

St. George Island, Florida

St. George Island, Florida

Dauphin Island, Alabama

Georgetown,
South Carolina

Georgetown, South Carolina

Georgetown, South Carolina

Georgetown, South Carolina

Dauphin Island, Alabama

Dauphin Island,
Alabama

Natchez, Mississippi

Natchez, Mississippi

Natchez, Mississippi

Natchez, Mississippi

Natchez, Mississippi

Natchez,
Mississippi

Natchez, Mississippi

Emerald Mound on the Natchez Trace

Ancestors of the Natchez Indians built this ceremonial mound about 1400. The nation's second largest of its type, it covers nearly eight acres. A trail leads to the top.

Website: www.nps.gov/natr

Natchez Trace, Mississippi

Natchez Trace, Mississippi

Jackson, Mississippi

Natchez Trace, Mississippi

Port Gibson, Mississippi

Kosciuski, Mississippi

Port Gibson, Mississippi

Kosciuski, Mississippi

Port Gibson, Mississippi

Oxford, Mississippi – Rowan Oak, William Faulkner's home

Henning, Tennessee – boyhood home of Alex Haley, author of *Roots*

Bellview, Tennessee – Red Caboose Park

Nashville, Tennessee

Nashville, Tennessee

Jackson, Tennessee –
home of America's
railroad legend, Casey
Jones. A 130-ton
engine is on display
near the home
(www.caseyjones.com)

Belle Meade Plantation

Belle Meade Plantation is a nineteenth century thoroughbred horse farm. The plantation features living history, an 1853 Greek Revival Mansion, and seven other historic outbuildings.

Website: www.bellemeadeplantation.com

Nashville, Tennessee

Nashville, Tennessee – Belle Meade Plantation

Nashville, Tennessee

President James Monroe's home, Ash Lawn-Highland

Ash Lawn-Highland is a 535-acre estate with the atmosphere of a working plantation. Visitors enjoy President James Monroe's refurbished home and its American and French furnishings, costumed crafters, boxwood gardens, picnic spots, grazing cattle, and glimpses of Monticello.

Website: www.ashlawnhighland.org

Ashlawn-Highland, home of President James Monroe

Ashlawn-Highland, home of President James Monroe

Ashlawn-Highland, home of President James Monroe

Ashlawn-Highland, home of President James Monroe

Gunston Hall Plantation

Built in 1755, Gunston Hall was the colonial plantation home of George Mason, author of the Virginia Declaration of Rights and a framer of the United States Constitution. The house and gardens overlook the Potomac River.

Website: www.gunstonhall.org

Mason Neck, Virginia – entrance to Gunston Hall

Mason Neck, Virginia – Gunston Hall

Mason Neck, Virginia – Gunston Hall

Mason Neck, Virginia – Gunston Hall

Mason Neck, Virginia – Gunston Hall

107

Gettysburg, Pennsylvania

Gettysburg, Pennsylvania – About 2400 feet of historic fences are being built by volunteers in the Gettysburg National Military Park. These are part of the park's battlefield rehabilitation efforts to bring back missing features that affected the fighting in 1863.

Hanover, Pennsylvania

Florida

Florida Keys

Florida Keys

Florida Keys

Florida Keys

Florida Keys

Florida Keys

Florida Keys

Florida Keys

Lookout Mountain, Tennessee

Florida Keys

South Carolina

Myrtle Beach, South Carolina

McClellanville,
South Carolina –
Hampton
Plantation State
Historic Site

Myrtle Beach, South Carolina

Charleston, South Carolina

Charleston, South Carolina

Charleston, South Carolina

St. George Island, Florida

Charleston, South Carolina

South Carolina

St. George Island, Florida

St. George Island, Florida

St. George Island, Florida

St. George Island, Florida

St. George Island, Florida

Panama City Beach, Florida

Florida Gulf Coast

Panama City Beach,
Florida

Beautiful white sandy beach of the Florida Gulf Coast

Panama City Beach,
Florida

Dauphin Island, Alabama

Dauphin Island, Alabama

Biloxi, Mississippi

Dauphin Island, Alabama

New Orleans, Louisiana

Dauphin Island, Alabama

New Orleans, Louisiana

Mississippi

Louisiana

Mississippi

Tennessee

Canton, Mississippi

Nashville, Tennessee

Tennessee

Nashville, Tennessee

Nashville,
Tennessee

117

Gettysburg, Pennsylvania

Pennsylvania

Pennsylvania

118

Wood or Wood Appearing Fences and Gates Combined with Stone, Masonry, or Concrete

Awendaw, South Carolina

South Carolina

Awendaw, South Carolina

Drayton Hall Plantation

Built between 1738 and 1742, this plantation is preserved in its original state. Drayton Hall has never seen plumbing or central heat; it never had gas installed for lighting or heating purposes. The structure remains almost untouched as an eloquent statement about eighteenth century thinking, craftsmanship, technology, and design.

Website: www.draytonhall.org

Charleston, South Carolina – Magnolia Plantation

Charleston, South Carolina – Drayton Hall Plantation

Charleston, South Carolina – Magnolia Plantation

Magnolia Plantation

Magnolia Plantation is the original and continuing home of the Drayton family, owned now by a ninth-generation descendant. The house and famous lavish gardens are open daily.

Website: www.magnoliaplantation.com

New Orleans, Louisiana

Charleston, South Carolina – Magnolia Plantation

Panama City Beach

Mississippi

Panama City Beach

Canton, Mississippi

President Dwight D. Eisenhower

General and Mrs. Dwight D. Eisenhower owned only one home, their Gettysburg farm. They purchased it in 1950 after a thirty-year military career that took them around the world. During his two terms as president, Eisenhower used the farm as a weekend retreat and "temporary White House." In 1961, the farm became Eisenhower's retirement home.

Website: www.nps.gov/eise/

Gettysburg, Pennsylvania – Dwight D. Eisenhower ranch

Gettysburg, Pennsylvania – Dwight D. Eisenhower ranch

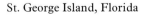

St. George Island, Florida

St. George Island, Florida

Jerry Lee Lewis

The home of rock 'n' roll legend Jerry Lee Lewis features memorabilia, a piano shaped swimming pool and The Killer Kar Kollection.

Nesbit, Mississippi – Jerry Lee Lewis ranch

Nesbit, Mississippi – Jerry Lee Lewis ranch

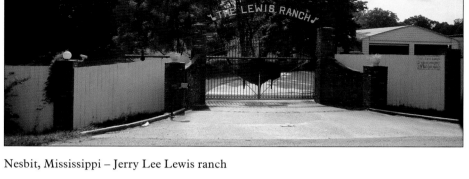

Nesbit, Mississippi – Jerry Lee Lewis ranch

Florida Keys

Florida Keys

Florida Keys

Florida Keys

Florida Keys

Florida Keys

Florida Keys

Florida Keys

Georgetown, South Carolina

Myrtle Beach, South Carolina

South Carolina

South Carolina

South Carolina

Charleston,
South Carolina

Charleston, South Carolina

Charleston, South Carolina

Charleston, South Carolina

Charleston, South Carolina

Charleston, South
Carolina

Canton, Mississippi

Chapter 6
Fences and Gates in Places of Special Interest

In Chapters 1 through 5, fences and gates were sorted according to the materials used in their construction. This chapter contains places of interest where there may be various styles of fences and/or gates used. Brief information about each location has also been included.

Beauvoir, Jefferson Davis Presidential Library and Home – Biloxi, Mississippi

Located between Biloxi and Handsboro, Mississippi, the Jefferson Davis Home and Presidential Library is a National Historic Landmark and a Mississippi Historic Landmark. The Presidential Library opened in 1998. Today, the historic site encompasses fifty-one acres of the original Beauvoir estate.

Website: www.beauvoir.org

Biloxi, Mississippi – Beauvoir, Jefferson Davis home and Presidential Library

Biloxi, Mississippi – Beauvoir, Jefferson Davis home and Presidential Library

Biloxi, Mississippi – Beauvoir, Jefferson Davis home and Presidential Library

Biloxi, Mississippi – Beauvoir, Jefferson Davis home and Presidential Library

Vicksburg, Mississippi – Belle of the Bends

Belle of the Bends – Vicksburg, Mississippi

Belle of the Bends, c. 1876, is located in the historic garden district of Vicksburg and is an example of Italianate architecture. It is furnished with family heirlooms, some of which are original to the mansion. Tours of the home are offered, including six unoccupied guest rooms and a history of the home and area.

Website: www.belleofthebends.com

Vicksburg, Mississippi – Belle of the Bends

Vicksburg, Mississippi – Belle of the Bends

Vicksburg, Mississippi
– Belle of the Bends

Vicksburg, Mississippi – Belle of the Bends

Vicksburg, Mississippi – Belle of the Bends

Brookgreen Gardens – Murrells Inlet, South Carolina

A place of great natural beauty, Brookgreen Gardens is on the site of what was once four plantations and includes botanical gardens, a wildlife park, pontoon cruises, and freshwater swamps. The property extends from the beach on the Atlantic Ocean to the swamps along the Waccamaw River. The gardens are laid out like separate rooms using the brick "walls" shown in the photos below. There are more than 550 nineteenth- and twentieth-century sculptures and more continue to be added.

Website: www.brookgreen.org

Murrells Inlet, South Carolina – Brookgreen Gardens

Murrells Inlet, South Carolina – Brookgreen Gardens

Murrells Inlet, South Carolina
– Brookgreen Gardens

Murrells Inlet, South Carolina – Brookgreen Gardens

Murrells Inlet, South Carolina – Brookgreen Gardens

Murrells Inlet, South Carolina –
Brookgreen Gardens

Murrells Inlet, South Carolina – Brookgreen Gardens

Cedar Grove Mansion – Vicksburg, Mississippi

A 33-room, c. 1840 Greek Revival mansion, Cedar Grove Mansion overlooks the Mississippi River. There are four acres of formal gardens, and the mansion is furnished with original antiques. A Union cannonball is still lodged in the parlor wall. It is operating as a historic bed and breakfast inn.

Website: www.cedargroveinn.com

Vicksburg, Mississippi – Cedar Grove Mansion

Vicksburg, Mississippi – Cedar Grove Mansion

Vicksburg, Mississippi – Cedar Grove Mansion

Vicksburg, Mississippi – Cedar Grove Mansion

Vicksburg, Mississippi – Cedar Grove Mansion

Vicksburg, Mississippi – Cedar Grove Mansion

Vicksburg, Mississippi – Cedar Grove Mansion

Near New Orleans, Louisiana – Destrehan Plantation

Destrehan Plantation – Destrehan, Louisiana

Built in French Colonial style, the c. 1787 Destrehan Manor House was remodeled to Greek Revival style in 1840. It is the oldest documented plantation house in the lower Mississippi River Valley, having survived colonial and civil wars plus the perils of time. In 1861, the Union Army seized the plantation and established the Rost Home Colony for the purpose of teaching trade skills to newly freed slaves. The house is currently furnished with antiques of the early 1800s.

Website: www.destrehanplantation.org

Near New Orleans, Louisiana – Destrehan Plantation

Near New Orleans, Louisiana – Destrehan Plantation

Near New Orleans, Louisiana – Destrehan Plantation

Near New Orleans, Louisiana – Destrehan Plantation

Near New Orleans, Louisiana – Destrehan Plantation

Near New Orleans, Louisiana –
Destrehan Plantation

Dunleith Plantation – Natchez, Mississippi

This 26-room, c. 1856 Greek Revival "temple" is completely surrounded by colonnaded galleries. It is located on a 40-acre landscaped park and boasts an array of outbuildings associated with antebellum life on a suburban estate. It is operating as a historic bed and breakfast inn.

Website: www.dunleithplantation.com

Natchez, Mississippi – Dunleith Plantation

Natchez, Mississippi – Dunleith Plantation

Natchez, Mississippi – Dunleith Plantation

Natchez, Mississippi – Dunleith Plantation

Natchez, Mississippi – Dunleith Plantation

Natchez, Mississippi – Dunleith Plantation

Fort Gaines – Dauphin Island, Mobile Bay, Alabama

Fort Gaines was established c. 1821 for defense of Mobile Bay and named in honor of General Edmund Pendleton Gaines, 1777-1849, who played an important part in early Alabama history. Located on the eastern tip of Dauphin Island, the fort was part of an extensive system of defenses built by the Confederates around Mobile in January 1861. Fort Gaines was involved in the Battle of Mobile Bay in 1864.

Website: www.dauphinisland.org/fort.htm

Dauphin Island near Mobile, Alabama – Fort Gaines

Dauphin Island near Mobile, Alabama – Fort Gaines

Dauphin Island near Mobile, Alabama – Fort Gaines

Memphis, Tennessee – Graceland, Elvis Presley's home

Graceland, Elvis Presley's Home – Memphis, Tennessee

Graceland was Elvis Presley's Memphis home until his death in 1977. Scores of fans visit the gate and block wall fence in front of his home. They have penned so many sentiments to "The King of Rock and Roll" on the block wall fence that many are written on top of each other in several layers.

Website: www.elvis.com

Memphis, Tennessee – Graceland, Elvis Presley's Home

Memphis, Tennessee – Graceland, Elvis Presley's home

Memphis, Tennessee – Graceland, Elvis Presley's home

Memphis, Tennessee – Graceland, Elvis Presley's home

136

Hermitage, Andrew Jackson's Plantation – Nashville, Tennessee

The Hermitage mansion was built between 1819 and 1821 and remodeled in 1831, including the addition of a one-story colonnade of ten columns. The Hermitage property ranged in size from 425 acres at its purchase in 1804 to 1,000 acres at Jackson's death in 1845.

Website: www.thehermitage.com

Nashville, Tennessee – Hermitage, Andrew Jackson's plantation

Nashville, Tennessee – Hermitage, Andrew Jackson's Plantation

Nashville, Tennessee – Hermitage, Andrew Jackson's plantation

Nashville, Tennessee – Hermitage, Andrew Jackson's plantation

137

Nashville, Tennessee – Hermitage, Andrew Jackson's plantation

Nashville, Tennessee – Hermitage, Andrew Jackson's plantation

Nashville, Tennessee – Hermitage, Andrew Jackson's plantation

Nashville, Tennessee – Hermitage, Andrew Jackson's plantation

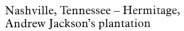

Nashville, Tennessee – Hermitage, Andrew Jackson's plantation

Nashville, Tennessee – Hermitage, Andrew Jackson's plantation

138

Nashville, Tennessee – Hermitage, Andrew Jackson's plantation

Nashville, Tennessee – Hermitage, Andrew Jackson's Plantation

---

Loretta Lynn Ranch – Hurricane Mills, Tennessee

Loretta Lynn's ranch includes Loretta's plantation home, an 18,000 square foot museum, a western town, a replica of Loretta's childhood home in Van Lear, Kentucky, a simulated coal mine, a campground, a concert pavilion, and much more.

Website: www.lorettalynn.com

Hurricane Mills, Tennessee – Loretta Lynn ranch

Nashville, Tennessee – Hermitage, Andrew Jackson's Plantation

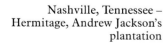

Nashville, Tennessee – Hermitage, Andrew Jackson's plantation

Hurricane Mills, Tennessee – Loretta Lynn ranch

Hurricane Mills, Tennessee – Loretta Lynn ranch

Hurricane Mills, Tennessee – Loretta Lynn ranch

Hurricane Mills, Tennessee – Loretta Lynn ranch

Hurricane Mills, Tennessee – Loretta Lynn ranch

Hurricane Mills, Tennessee – Loretta Lynn ranch

Hurricane Mills, Tennessee – Loretta Lynn ranch

Charleston, South Carolina – Middleton Place

Charleston, South Carolina – Middleton Place

Middleton Place – Plantation near Charleston, South Carolina
　　Middleton Place is an elegant plantation near Charleston on the Ashley River. It was the home of Henry Middleton, president of the First Continental Congress, and his son Arthur, a signer of the Declaration of Independence.
　　Website: www.middletonplace.org

Charleston, South Carolina – Middleton Place

Charleston, South Carolina – Middleton Place

Monticello, Thomas Jefferson's Home – Charlottesville, Virginia

Monticello is the only house in America designated as a United Nations World Heritage site. Thomas Jefferson inherited the 5,000-acre plantation from his father, Peter Jefferson, in 1764. It was home to Jefferson, his extended family, and as many as 150 slaves. Thomas Jefferson is buried at Monticello with other members of his family in a graveyard chosen by him in 1773.

Website: www.monticello.org

Charlottesville, Virginia – Monticello, Thomas Jefferson's home

Charlottesville, Virginia – Monticello, Thomas Jefferson's home

Charlottesville, Virginia – Monticello, Thomas Jefferson's home

Charlottesville, Virginia – Monticello, Thomas Jefferson's home

Charlottesville, Virginia – Monticello, Thomas Jefferson's home

Charlottesville, Virginia – Monticello, Thomas Jefferson's home

Charlottesville, Virginia – Monticello, Thomas Jefferson's home

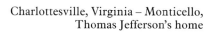

Charlottesville, Virginia – Monticello,
Thomas Jefferson's home

Charlottesville, Virginia – Monticello, Thomas Jefferson's home

Charlottesville, Virginia – Monticello, Thomas Jefferson's home

Mount Vernon, George Washington's Home – Virginia, south of Washington, D.C.

Mount Vernon was granted to George Washington's great-grandfather in 1674 and passed down in the family until he acquired it by lease in 1754. Washington worked tirelessly for nearly half a century to expand his plantation to 8,000 acres and improve the appearance of the mansion, outbuildings, and extensive gardens and grounds. He died in 1799 and is entombed at Mount Vernon. The Washington family continued to live at Mount Vernon until 1858. At that time, the estate and 200 acres were purchased by the Mount Vernon Ladies' Association. This organization continues to operate Mount Vernon today.

Website: www.mountvernon.org

Virginia, south of Washington, D.C. – Mount Vernon, George Washington's plantation

Virginia, south of Washington, D.C. – Mount Vernon, George Washington's plantation

Virginia, south of Washington, D.C. – Mount Vernon, George Washington's plantation

Virginia, south of Washington, D.C. – Mount Vernon, George Washington's plantation

Virginia, south of Washington, D.C. – Mount Vernon, George Washington's plantation

Virginia south of Washington, D.C. – Mount Vernon, George Washington's plantation

Virginia, south of Washington, D.C. – Mount Vernon, George Washington's plantation

Virginia, south of Washington, D.C. – Mount Vernon, George Washington's plantation

Virginia, south of Washington, D.C. – Mount Vernon, George Washington's plantation

Virginia, south of Washington, D.C. – Mount Vernon, George Washington's plantation

Virginia, south of Washington, D.C. – Mount Vernon, George Washington's plantation

As this sign at Mount Vernon explains, "Washington attempted to replace his expensive wood fences with 'live' fences—hedges so dense that they would turn away all animals, from the smallest rabbit to the largest deer. Despite his repeated directions to plant the banks of ditches with fast-growing locust and willow, he never succeeded in fully protecting his garden harvest with live fences."

Virginia, south of Washington, D.C. – Mount Vernon, George Washington's plantation

Virginia, south of Washington, D.C. – Mount Vernon, George Washington's plantation

Virginia, south of Washington, D.C. – Mount Vernon, George Washington's plantation

Virginia, south of Washington, D.C. – Mount Vernon, George Washington's plantation

Virginia, south of Washington, D.C. – Mount Vernon, George Washington's plantation

Virginia, south of Washington, D.C. – Mount Vernon, George Washington's plantation

National Ornamental Metal Museum – Memphis, Tennessee

This book would not be complete without including the National Ornamental Metal Museum in Memphis, Tennessee. The impressive Anniversary Gates at the entrance to the museum were dedicated in 1989 to celebrate the tenth anniversary of the museum's opening. The detail photos show some of the rosettes created by two hundred metal smiths worldwide. Museum exhibitions vary and include a full range of metalwork, from functional objects to precious jewelry to contemporary sculpture.

Website: www.metalmuseum.org

Memphis, Tennessee – National Ornamental Metal Museum

Memphis, Tennessee – National Ornamental Metal Museum

Memphis, Tennessee –
National Ornamental
Metal Museum

Memphis, Tennessee – National Ornamental Metal Museum

Memphis, Tennessee – National Ornamental Metal Museum

Memphis, Tennessee – National
Ornamental Metal Museum

Memphis, Tennessee –
National Ornamental
Metal Museum

Memphis, Tennessee – National Ornamental Metal
Museum

Memphis, Tennessee –
National Ornamental
Metal Museum

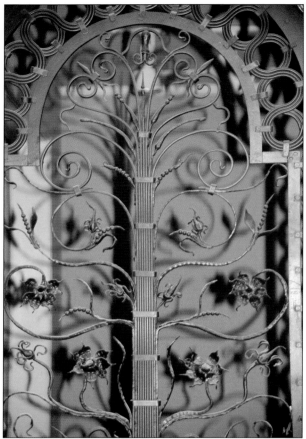

Memphis, Tennessee – National Ornamental Metal Museum

Memphis, Tennessee – National Ornamental Metal Museum

Memphis, Tennessee – National Ornamental Metal Museum

Memphis, Tennessee – National Ornamental Metal Museum

Memphis, Tennessee – National Ornamental Metal Museum

Memphis, Tennessee – National Ornamental Metal Museum

Memphis, Tennessee – National Ornamental Metal Museum

Memphis, Tennessee – National Ornamental Metal Museum

Memphis, Tennessee – National Ornamental Metal Museum

151

The White House – Washington, D.C.

Visit the website below for online shows and tours of the White House. The website is presented by the White House Historical Association.

Website: www.whitehousehistory.org

Washington, D.C.,
The White House

Washington, D.C., The White House

Washington, D.C.,
The White House

Washington, D.C., The White House

Washington, D.C., The White House